Contents

Published by
Boston Music Company

Exclusive Distributors:
Music Sales Corporation
257 Park Avenue South, New York, NY10010, USA.
Music Sales Limited
8/9 Frith Street, London W1D 3JB, England.
Music Sales Pty Limited
120 Rothschild Avenue, Rosebery, NSW 2018, Australia.

This book © Copyright 2006 Boston Music Company,
a division of Music Sales Corporation

Edited by David Harrison
Music processed by Paul Ewers Music Design
Original compositions and arrangements by Brian Thomson
Cover and book designed by Chloë Alexander
Photography by Matthew Ward
Models: Chigozie Nri and Heidi Sutcliffe
Printed in the United States of America
 by Vicks Lithograph and Printing Corporation
Backing tracks by Guy Dagul
CD performance by Brian Thomson
CD recorded, mixed and mastered by Jonas Persson and John Rose

Your Guarantee of Quality
As publishers, we strive to produce every book to the highest commercial
standards. The music has been freshly engraved and the book has been
carefully designed to minimize awkward page turns and to make playing
from it a real pleasure. Throughout, the printing and binding have been
planned to ensure a sturdy, attractive publication which should give years
of enjoyment. If your copy fails to meet our high standards, please inform
us and we will gladly replace it.

www.musicsales.com

Rudiments of music

The staff

Music is written on a grid of five lines called a *staff*.
At the beginning of each staff is placed a special symbol called a *clef* to describe the approximate range of the instrument for which the music is written.

This example shows a *treble clef*, generally used for melody instruments.

The staff is divided into equal sections of time, called *bars* or *measures*, by *barlines*.

Note values

Different symbols are used to show the time value of *notes*, and each *note value* has an equivalent symbol for a rest, representing silence.

The **eighth note**, often used to signify a half beat, is written with a solid head and a stem with a tail. The eighth-note rest is also shown.

The **quarter note**, often used to signify one beat, is written with a solid head and a stem. The quarter-note rest is also shown.

The **half note** is worth two quarter notes. It is written with a hollow head and a stem. The half-note rest is placed on the middle line.

The **whole note** is worth two half notes. It is written with a hollow head. The whole-note rest hangs from the fourth line.

Other note values

Note values can be increased by half by adding a dot after the note head. Here a half note and quarter note are together worth a *dotted* half note.

Grouping eighth notes

Where two or more eighth notes follow each other, they can be joined by a *beam* from stem to stem.

Time signatures

The number of beats in a bar is determined by the *time signature*, a pair of numbers placed after the clef.
The upper number shows how many beats each bar contains, while the lower number indicates what kind of note value
is used to represent a single beat. This lower number is a fraction of a whole note, so that 4 represents quarter notes
and 8 represents eighth notes.

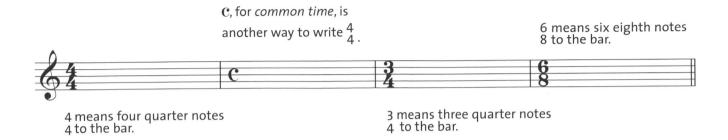

C, for *common time*, is another way to write $\frac{4}{4}$.

6 means six eighth notes 8 to the bar.

4 means four quarter notes 4 to the bar.

3 means three quarter notes 4 to the bar.

Note names

Notes are named after the first seven letters of the alphabet and are written on lines or spaces on the staff,
according to pitch.

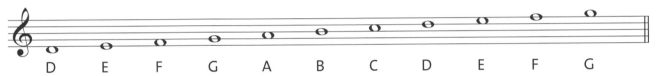

D E F G A B C D E F G

Accidentals

The pitch of a note can be altered up or down a half step (or *semitone*) by the use of sharp and flat symbols.
These temporary pitch changes are known as *accidentals*.

The *sharp* (♯) raises the pitch of a note.

The *natural* (♮) returns the note to its original pitch.

The *flat* (♭) lowers the pitch of a note.

Ledger lines

Ledger lines are used to extend the range of the staff for low or high notes.

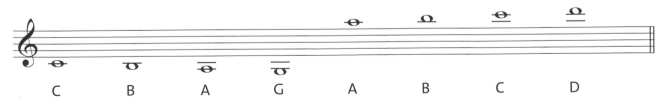

C B A G A B C D

Barlines

Various different types of barlines are used:
Double barlines divide one section of music from another.

Final barlines show the end of a piece of music.

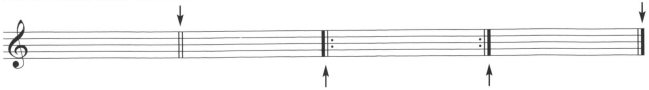

Repeat marks show a section to be repeated.

Before you play:

The trumpet and accessories

Your complete trumpet outfit should include the following:

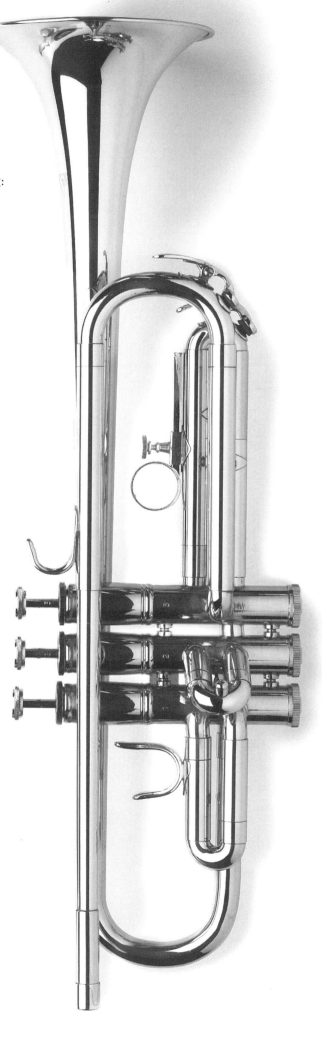

• Mouthpiece

• Valve oil

• Duster

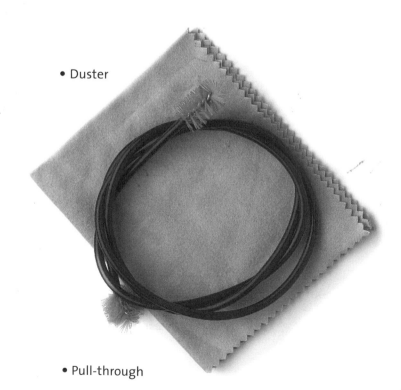

• Pull-through

Setting-up routine

Place the mouthpiece into the receiver and check that the valves and slides are all free – a few drops of oil on each valve every other day and a little grease on the slides occasionally will keep everything moving freely.

Remove the mouthpiece again before putting your instrument away.

Maintenance

Give your instrument a bath now and again – it will play much better if it is clean on the inside.

Strip the instrument down and immerse it in luke warm soapy water with a little disinfectant.

Pull the long brush through the leadpipe and all the slides. Rinse with luke warm water then dry it with a soft towel – remember to oil the valves and grease the slides afterwards.

Use a soft duster to keep your instrument clean and shiny.

Practice

Playing any musical instrument is a physical skill, and repetition is necessary to develop your mental and muscular skills. The three most important things to remember about practice are:

1. Practice until you can't get something wrong, rather than just until you get it right once; this way you are less likely to get it wrong next time.

2. It is much better to practice "little and often" rather than in one long session once a week. A daily practice routine of 15 or 20 minutes is ideal.

3. Never finish a practice session without having gotten at least one thing better than it was when you started.

Lesson 1 — goals:

1. **Breathing using the diaphragm**
2. **Posture**
3. **Formation of the mouth shape (embouchure)**
4. **Buzzing on the mouthpiece**
5. **Making a sound on the instrument**

Breathing

A relaxed, controlled posture is essential for comfort and correct breathing.

When breathing in and out, always use your diaphragm. This is a large muscular membrane underneath your rib cage which causes your stomach to go *out* when breathing in and to go *in* when breathing out.

You will be able to control your breathing far more effectively using your diaphragm than if you were to breathe with the *intercostal* muscles high up in your chest.

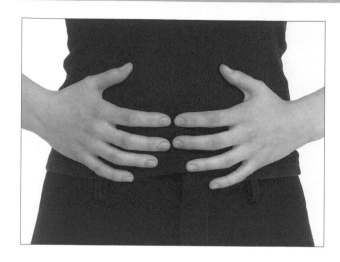

Exercise 1:

Count a steady beat in your head as you inhale through your nose then exhale naturally through your mouth. Feel the air going deep down into your lungs.

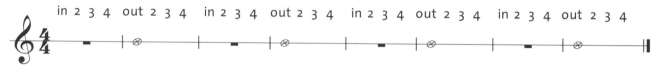

in 2 3 4   out 2 3 4   in 2 3 4   out 2 3 4   in 2 3 4   out 2 3 4   in 2 3 4   out 2 3 4

All good trumpet players take a deep breath every time they play.

Posture

Stand up tall with your feet planted shoulder width apart.

Keep this posture as you raise the trumpet to playing position, allowing your elbows to move forward and away from your body. Keep the shoulders relaxed.

Hold the weight of the trumpet with the left hand while keeping the right hand relaxed for a good valve technique.

Wrap your **left hand** around the valves using one finger to operate the 3rd valve slide (the slide with the ring mounted above it). Depending on the size of your hand, either the ring finger or little finger will fit into the ring.

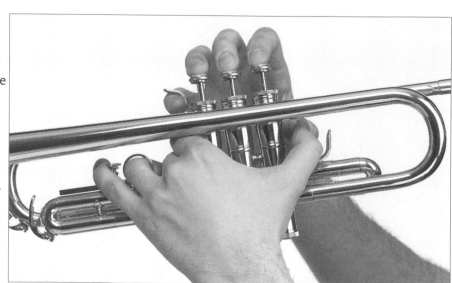

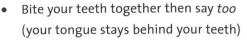

Embouchure

Follow this routine to set up your embouchure correctly:

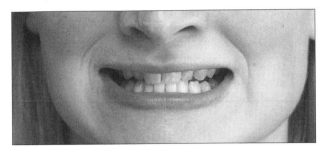

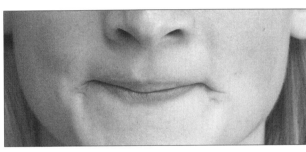

- Bite your teeth together then say *too*
  (your tongue stays behind your teeth)

- Now open your teeth slightly (just enough to
  let some air through)

- Inhale as you say *emmmm* (this compresses
  your lips – hold the "mmm")

- Blow... As you spit *tffff*
  (enjoy blowing raspberries!)

*Try moistening your
lips before you play to
help free the "buzz."*

Placing the mouthpiece

The mouthpiece should ideally be placed in the center
with half on the upper lip and half on the lower lip.

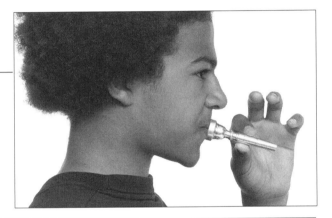

Buzzing on the mouthpiece

Try this exercise using only the mouthpiece.

Exercise 2:

Listen to CD tracks 3 and 4. Try to home in on one of these notes while "buzzing" this exercise.

Aim for whichever note feels more comfortable.

Now, place the mouthpiece in the trumpet and do exactly the same.

3–4

Exercise 3:

Take a deep breath and enjoy the sound!
Practice this many times.

You will naturally play either a **G** or a **C**.

> ### N O T E
> If your preferred note is **G** proceed to
> lesson **1G** on page 12.
> If you are more comfortable
> playing a **C** begin with lesson **1C** on page 10.

goals:

1. Tonguing
2. The notes C and D
3. Counting while playing: quarter notes, half notes, and whole notes
4. Little C & D march

The note C

First practice playing a nice steady **C**.

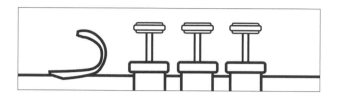

Breathe and blow *tffff*.

Exercise 1:

Listen to the sound.

Breathe in while counting 4 beats, then play for 4 beats, and so on.

Now let's try tonguing a few notes. Say *too* for each note, like so:

Exercise 2:

Take a deep breath and blow.

Try to feel a regular pulse as you play.

Exercise 3:

Exercise 4:

Exercise 5:

The note D

Now do exactly the same with the note **D**.

D is played using the 1st & 3rd valves.

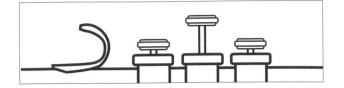

Raise the trumpet to your lips – and try not to stoop!

Exercise 6:

Exercise 7: Take a deep breath and blow.

Now try these tunes using C and D.

Tune 1:

Tune 2:

Tune 3:

Play this exercise by tonguing only the first note of each group.

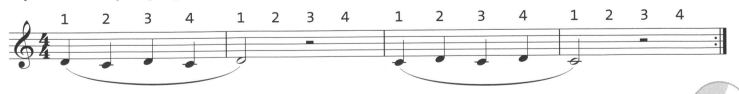

Little C & D March: Take a deep breath and blow.

5●6

Now proceed to Lesson **2C** on page 14.

11

1. **Tonguing**
2. **The notes G and F**
3. **Counting while playing: quarter notes, half notes, and whole notes**
4. **Little F & G march**

The note G

First practice playing a nice steady **G**.

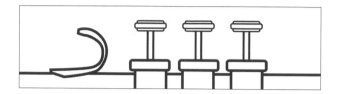

Breathe and blow *tffff*.

Exercise 1:

Listen to the sound.

Breathe in while counting 4 beats, then play for 4 beats, and so on.

Now let's try tonguing a few notes. Say *too* for each note, like so:

Exercise 2:

Take a deep breath and blow.

Try to feel a regular pulse as you play.

Exercise 3:

Exercise 4:

Exercise 5:

The note F

Now do exactly the same with the note **F**.

F is played using the 1st valve.

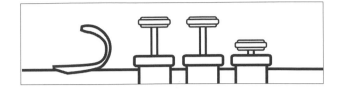

Raise the trumpet to your lips – and try not to stoop!

Exercise 6:

in 2 3 4 blow 2 3 4 in 2 3 4 blow 2 3 4 in 2 3 4 blow 2 3 4

Exercise 7: Take a deep breath and blow.

1 2 3 4 1 2 3 4 1 2 3 4 1 2 3 4

Now try these tunes using F and G.

Tune 1:

1 2 3 4 1 2 3 4 1 2 3 4 1 2 3 4

Tune 2:

1 2 3 4 1 2 3 4 1 2 3 4 1 2 3 4

Tune 3:

Play this exercise by tonguing only the first note of each group.

1 2 3 4 1 2 3 4 1 2 3 4 1 2 3 4

Little F & G March: Take a deep breath and blow.

7●8

Now proceed to Lesson **2G** on page 15.

goals:

1. The notes E & F

The note E

The note E is played using the 1st & 2nd valves.

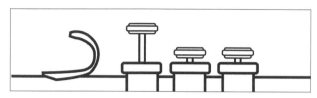

The note F

The note F is played using the 1st valve.

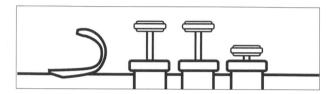

Exercise 1: Take a deep breath and blow.

Exercise 2:

Try to learn both parts.

Duet

Now work through lessons **1G** and **2G** before playing the pieces for Lesson 2.

goals:

1. The notes E & D

The note E

The note E is played using the 1st & 2nd valves.

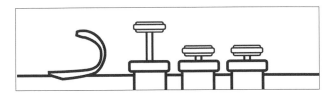

The note D

The note D is played using the 1st & 3rd valves.

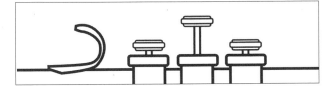

Exercise 1: Take a deep breath and blow.

Exercise 2:

Duet

Try to learn both parts.

Now work through lessons **1C** and **2C** before playing the pieces for Lesson 2.

15

Pieces for Lesson 2

Gheta Sea

Oats And Beans

11-12   ### *Lightly Row*

13   ### *Medieval Dance*

Try this canon with your teacher. The second player begins a bar after the first.
Notice the pause (or *fermata*) sign ⌢ . This means that the note is held, making it a little longer than
is written. The second player should finish on the pause in the penultimate bar.

Canon

Au Clair de la Lune

Going Cuckoo

Pia-Pia-Piano

1. Tied notes and slurred notes

Tied notes

So far we have tongued all our notes. Let's now introduce the *tie* and the *slur*.

Two notes of the same pitch can be joined together by *tying* them with a curved line.

This new note is held for the combined value of both notes, and the note can be held into the next bar.

Hold this note for 3 beats.   Hold the middle note for 2 beats.

Tongue Tied

Slurred notes

To play smoothly between different notes we *slur* from one to the next without using the tongue and using only the valves.

Ice Slur

Oats And Beans

Take care to spot which notes are *tied* and which ones are *slurred*.

Lightly Row

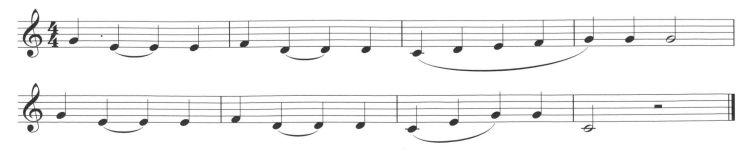

18

Pieces for Lesson 3

Upidee Duet

When The Saints Go Marching In

Up The Old Vic

goals:

1. **Tongue & fingers coordination**
2. **Time signatures**
3. **Slurred notes**
4. **Dotted notes**

Team talk

The tongue and fingers need to work together as a team, and to achieve smooth changes between notes it helps to move the valves quickly.

In the following exercises, *bang down* the valves as you tongue the notes.

Exercise 1:

1st time tongued, 2nd time slurred

Try the same exercise again with the slurs. Move the valves quickly to make it nice and smooth.

Gliding

Ice Is Nice

1st time tongued, 2nd time slurred

Dotted Notes

A dot placed to the right of a note multiplies its duration by half as much again.

For example both notes here have the same duration.

> **THINK!**
>
> Take a deep breath and blow through the slurs.
> Are you standing up straight?
> Don't slouch!

Time signatures

Everything you have played so far has had a **time signature** of four beats to every bar:

Many pieces, however, contain three beats per bar. This means that the counting will be:

Waltzes always use this time signature.

Pieces for Lesson 4

Floating Along

Be sure to count in time.

Dance

Sailing Along Duet

Learn both parts for this piece. Keep a steady beat.

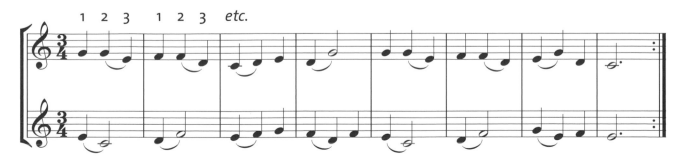

Lesson 5

goals:

1. **Lip slur**
2. **Vowel sounds**
3. **The notes A and B**
4. **Dynamics**

Lip slurs and vowel sounds

So far you have *slurred* between two notes using the valves.

We can also *lip slur* between two notes that use the same valves.
To help change the note it is useful to blow using vowel sounds.

For example, say *ah* then *eee*—feel the difference in the level of your tongue?
We use these vowel sounds and many in between to help our flexibility on the instrument.

Using the sounds *too – ah* and *ah – hoo,* try these exercises on the mouthpiece only as well as on the trumpet.

Exercise 1:

Remember to take a deep breath before blowing.

On the way down from G to C, move quickly between *oo – ah* and relax your lips slightly to achieve a nice clean lip slur.

Repeat these many times until it feels comfortable.

On the way up you'll need a bit of a push of air from your diaphragm.
Say *hoo*—feel where that push of air comes from? Think *tah – hoo* on the way up.

Exercise 2:

Blow through the lip slur.

On the way up from C to G, move quickly between *ah – hoo* and compress your lips slightly to achieve a nice clean lip slur.

Exercise 3:

Once this is comfortable, try the same exercise with the 2nd valve down.

You can play these exercises using any valve combination.
Ask your teacher to demonstrate!

22

The note A

The note A is played using the 1st & 2nd valves.

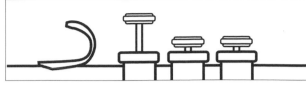

The note B

The note B is played using the 2nd valve in both the upper and lower registers.

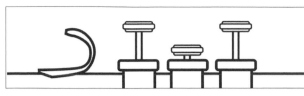

Extending range to A & B

Play these exercises first time tongued and second time all slurred.

Blow through the crescendos to give you some power for the higher notes.

Exercise 4:

1st time tongued, 2nd time slurred

Exercise 5:

1st time tongued, 2nd time slurred

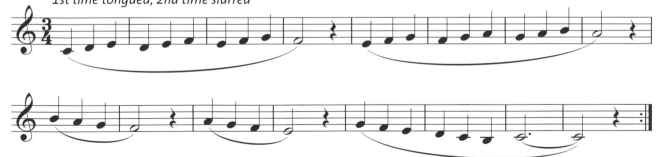

Dynamics

To play at a loud dynamic (*f* – *forte*) you must *blow* the air faster through the instrument, and to play quietly (*p* – *piano*) blow gently while keeping some air support from your diaphragm.

Crescendo means gradually get louder,

also shown as ◁——

Diminuendo means gradually get quieter,

also shown as ——▷

Pieces for Lesson 5

Call And Response

Play this fun piece with another player.

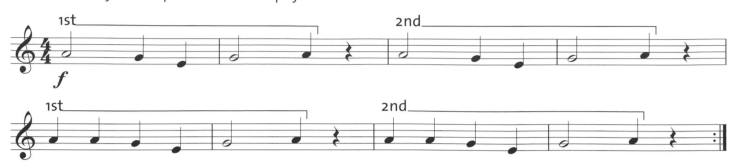

Twinkle Twinkle

Joshua Fought The Battle Of Jericho

26-27

Crusaders' Hymn

Pieces for Lesson 5

Steal Away

28-29

Happy Days

Try to play this one a little quicker and emphasize the beginning of each tied note to achieve a lively feel.

Blue Tuesday Duet

30

Learn both parts.

1. Note duration

On the staff below, draw notes of the indicated duration:

(4)

2. Rests

On the staff below, draw rests of the indicated duration:

(4)

3. Notes

On the staff below, draw the following notes as half notes:

G, B, E, C, A, D and **F**

(4)

4. Identity parade

Identify the following elements in this piece of music:

Quarter note, Barline, Time signature, Quarter-note rest, Tied note, Treble clef, Whole note, Dotted half note

(8)

5. Bars

Draw barlines on this staff where they are needed:

(5)

Total (25)

26

warm up:

As with any physical activity it is a good idea to *warm up* each day with a few simple exercises to loosen up the muscles, get the blood flowing and focus the mind.
Warming up helps to make each practice session more productive.

Develop a new good habit by warming up for five minutes each day with some simple exercises.
Ask your teacher for good advice on how to warm up. Here are some exercises to try:

1. Mouthpiece buzzing

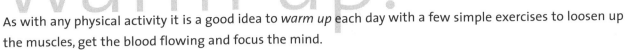

Buzz a few long steady notes and a few slides to free up the buzz.

2. Long notes

Play a few long notes and listen to the sound. Is it clear?

Is it a beautiful sound? Imagine you are blowing warm air into the trumpet. Try standing at the window and steam it up by blowing warm air onto it. Feel how this opens up your throat?

3. Lip slurs

4. Tonguing (Production)

Try to get good clean starts to each note.

GOOD BRASS HABITS

- Always take a deep breath, even to play a quiet note
- Breathe in time, being ready to blow when the note should begin
- Stand or sit with good posture: feet planted, shoulders down, back off the chair
- Raise the trumpet to your lips and try not to stoop
- Blow warm air, keeping your throat open

Lesson 6

goals:

1. The notes C, E♭ and B♭
2. C major scale
3. D.C. al Fine

The note C

You have already met the note C in the lower octave. Use the same fingering for the upper octave (open valves).

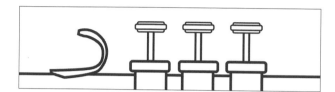

The scale of C major

A scale is a series of notes that move up or down by step from one note to the same note an octave higher or lower.

The note E♭

The note E♭ is played using the 2nd & 3rd valves.

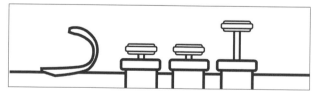

The note B♭

The note B♭ is played using the 1st valve.

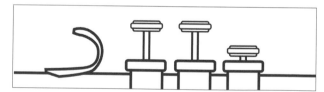

Pieces for Lesson 6

Skye Boat Song

This beautiful melody has *D.C. al Fine* written at the end. This means that you play all the way through then go back to the beginning and play through again until you see *Fine*.

Scarborough Fair Duet

33

Joshua Fought The Battle Of Jericho

goals:

1. Combine the up and down lip slur

Here are some exercises to help you play lip slurs in both directions.

Move quickly between the vowel sounds *ooo* and *ah* as you compress and relax your lips.

Blow more air (*hoo*) as you go higher.

Exercise 1:

Repeat these until they become comfortable.

Exercise 2:

Blow through the slur.

Now try these again using different valve combinations.

Now move down in semitones, starting on F♯ (2nd valve), then F (1st valve) and finally E (1st & 2nd valve).

Ask your teacher to demonstrate these.

Exercise 3:

Blow the vowel sounds to help push the lip slurs up and down.

GOOD BRASS HABITS

Practice lip slurs slowly at first.
Blow through the changes to make
them clean and smooth.

Pieces for Lesson 7

When The Saints Go Marching In

Yankee Doodle

Medieval Dance

Swap parts on the repeat.

Canon The Bells

The 2nd player begins one bar later and finishes on the first pause. Play this one quickly—think in two half-note beats to the bar.

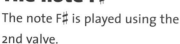

Lesson 8

goals:

1. **Warm up**
2. **The note F♯**
3. **Key of G major**

The note F♯

Don't forget to warm up.

Five minutes on these simple exercises will help you develop your playing in the right way and make your practice sessions more productive.

The note F♯ is played using the 2nd valve.

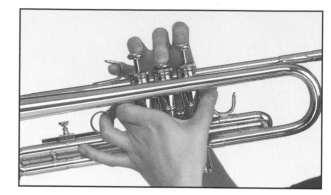

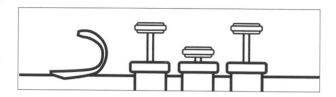

Exercise 1:

A sharp (♯) raises the note by a semitone and a flat (♭) lowers the note by a semitone.

A natural (♮) cancels out the effect of a sharp or a flat—simply play a natural note.

In this next exercise take care to play the correct sharp, flat or natural notes.

Exercise 2:

Key signatures

If you try to sing a simple tune such as *Somewhere Over The Rainbow*, you may find you can't reach the high notes without really straining. The solution is to start the piece a little lower.

This time, you may be able to sing the high notes more comfortably.

You are now singing in a different *key*.

There are many different keys in music, each of which needs its own set of notes.

The key of C major is easy as it requires no sharps or flats.

The key of G major has 1 sharp (F♯). Notice the sharp sign (♯) at the beginning of the staff—this means that every F throughout this piece is played as an F♯.

Exercise 3:

Pieces for Lesson 8

Au Clair de la Lune Duet

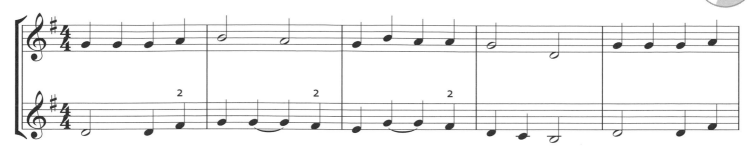

Jingle Bells

goals:

1. Eighth notes, 2/4 time signature & Common time

2. Anacrusis (Upbeat)

Eighth notes

Eighth notes are half the length of quarter notes so we play two eighths in the time of one quarter. And similarly the time signature of $\frac{2}{4}$ has half as many beats as $\frac{4}{4}$. Therefore the same melody can be played in $\frac{2}{4}$ using eighth notes as in $\frac{4}{4}$ using quarter notes.

The **C** at the start is an alternative way of writing the time signature $\frac{4}{4}$ and is called "common time."

Exercise 1:

Exercise 2:

Exercise 3:

Exercise 4:

Take care with the following exercise; note the *key signature* and *time signature*.

> ### THINK!
>
> Are you practicing properly?
> Remember, a little each day...
> Always warm up before you practice.
> Your session will be more productive,
> therefore you will progress at a
> quicker rate.

Pieces for Lesson 9

Abide With Me

Long, Long Ago

arranged Mayes

Anacrusis (upbeat)

Sometimes a piece of music doesn't begin with a whole bar. The next piece begins with a single beat representing the last beat of a bar. This short bar (called an *upbeat* or *anacrusis*) is balanced by another short bar at the end. The two short bars add up to a whole bar.

Remember – the symbol ⌢ above the last note in this next piece is called a **pause** or **fermata**.
It means you should hold the note for longer than its actual value of 3 beats.

Oh Come All Ye Faithful

Yankee Doodle

goals:

1. **Tonguing exercises**
2. **The upper note D**
3. **Key of F major**
4. **More Dynamics**

Tonguing exercises

Don't forget to warm up.

Try these exercises a little quicker each time.

Gradually speed them up without losing the quality of your note production.

Exercise 1:

Practice coordinating the valves and the tongue at gradually quicker tempos.

Exercise 2:

Key of F major

Notice that the key of F major has one flat (B♭), so all the Bs throughout this piece are played as B♭s.

Exercise 3:

The upper note D

The upper note D is played using the 1st valve.

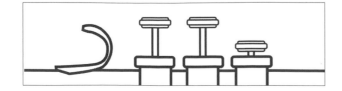

Exercise 4:

More dynamics

So far you have only learned two dynamics, soft (*p*) and loud (*f*). The letter *m* can be used in combination with *p* and *f* to create other dynamics: *mp* (*mezzo piano*) means moderately soft and *mf* (*mezzo forte*) means moderately loud. The Italian word *mezzo* means literally "half."

Exercise 5:

Play these notes with the indicated dynamics.

Pieces for Lesson 10

Hark! The Herald Angels Sing

44-45

Pieces for Lesson 10

46–47 *Auld Lang Syne*

48–49 *In Dulci Jubilo*

Jubilant

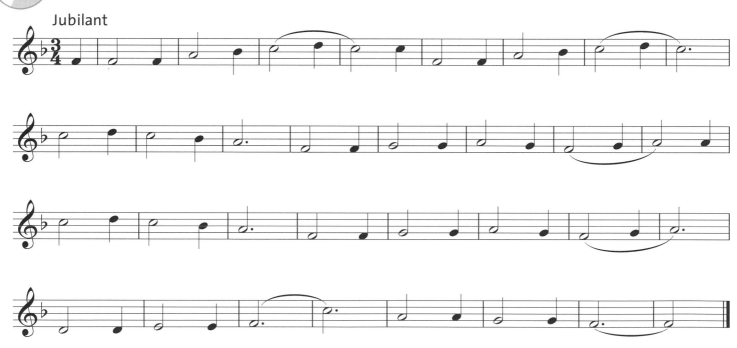

Listen to track 2 on the CD. Learn this next tune and you can play along at the beginning, on the repeat and during the final refrain of the recording.

2 *Prince Of Denmark's March*

test: *for* Lessons 6 to 10

1. Note duration

On the staff below, draw notes of the indicated duration:

one eighth note	2 beats' worth of eighth notes	dotted quarter note	a note that lasts for five eighth notes

(4)

2. Scale

On the staff below, draw the G major scale including the correct key signature:

(4)

3. Time signatures

Write in the correct time signature at the beginning of each bar:

(6)

4. Dynamics

What are the Italian words for:

Moderately loud _____

Moderately quiet _____

(4)

5. Performance

Choose your favorite piece so far and **perform** it to an audience of friends, family or your teacher.

(7)

Total **(25)**

39

goals:

1. **The note G♯**
2. **Minor keys**

3. **A minor scales**
4. **Staccato and tenuto tonguing**

The note G♯

We play the note G♯ using the 2nd valve.

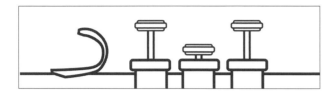

Exercise 1:

Remember – in any bar, a note that has been flatted or sharped will remain so throughout the bar unless indicated.

Minor keys and minor scales

You have already played many cheerful melodies in different major keys.

To play something that sounds sad or melancholic a **minor** key would more often be used.

C major and A minor share the same key signature since they are based on the same range of notes.
For this reason we call them *relatives*—A minor is the *relative* minor of C major.

All major keys have a relative minor key and there are two types of minor scales—melodic and harmonic.

Exercise 2:

In the *melodic minor scale* the notes change on the way down whereas they remain the *same both ways* in the *harmonic minor scale*.

40

Exercise 3:

Staccato & tenuto tonguing

Staccato tonguing means playing very short notes. Look out for the dot above or below the notehead.

Tenuto means playing long, full length notes. Look out for the line.

Exercise 4:

Play this exercise again using *tenuto* tonguing.

Try tonguing *doo doo doo* to achieve long, full notes and nice smooth changes.

Pieces for Lesson 11

Theme From Symphony No.9

Beethoven

Oh! Susannah

While Shepherds Watched Their Flocks

Gently

Lesson 12

goals:

1. The note C♯
2. Key of D major
3. D major scale

Don't forget to warm up.

The note bottom C♯

We play the note bottom C♯ using all 3 valves.

The note upper C♯

We play the upper C♯ on 1st & 2nd valves.

The scale of D major

Notice that the key of D major has two sharps (F♯ & C♯), so all the Fs and Cs will be sharp throughout the piece.

Exercise 1:

TALKING ITALIAN

Dolce means sweet.
Play the lullaby on the following page sweetly.

42

Pieces for Lesson 12

Deck The Halls

52–53

Lullaby

54

Joy To The World

55–56

1. **Triplets**
2. **⁶⁄₈ time signature**

Triplets & ⁶⁄₈ time signature

So far we have had two eighth notes to each quarter note. Let's have some fun with three.

These are called **triplets** since we play three notes to every beat like so:

Exercise 1:

The 3 above each group of notes tells us to play 3 notes in each beat.

The same rhythm could also be written like this:

Exercise 2:

Think: 1 & a 2 & a 1 & a 2 & a etc...

⁶⁄₈ means we have six eighth notes in each bar. Think of it as two beats in the bar, two groups of three.

Pieces for Lesson 13

Mexican Hat Dance

think!

Row, Row, Row Your Boat

Pieces for Lesson 13

Mulberry Bush

57–58

Spanish Dance

59–60

Lean on the tied notes to give this one some Spanish flavor.

On Christmas Night

goals:

1. **Key of B♭ major**
2. **Scale of B♭ major**
3. **Introduction to swing eighths**
4. **D.S. al Fine**

Let's have some more fun with some jazz-style triplets.

Jazzy tunes have a natural triplet rhythm with a "swinging" feel, like so:

Exercise 1:

Exercise 2:

The same piece would more often be written like this, with "Swing" written above:

Key of B♭

Notice that the key of B♭ has two flats (B♭ and E♭), so all the Bs throughout this piece are played as B♭s, and all the Es are E♭s.

> **REMEMBER!**
>
> B♭ is played with the 1st valve, and E♭ is played with the 2nd and 3rd valves.

The scale of B♭ major

Pieces for Lesson 14

Blue Bells Of Scotland

Don't forget to warm up!

D.S. al Fine means go back to the sign (𝄋) and play again until *Fine* (end).

Jingle Bells – Jazz Style

Blow The Boogie Woogie

Believe Me If All Those Endearing Young Charms

goals:

1. **Lip slurs up to middle C**
2. **Lip flexibilities using all 7 valve combinations**

Lip Slurs

So far we have looked at lip slurs from C to G and below. Now lets try slurring using the next harmonic up.

Exercise 1:

Blow *too – hee.*

Feel what happens to your tongue?
And listen to the air speed increase!

Do exactly the same on the trumpet!

Exercise 2:

Let's begin with E on 1&2 and lip slur up to A. Use a slightly higher vowel sound for this one.

Always remember to take a deep breath.

Blow through the slur.

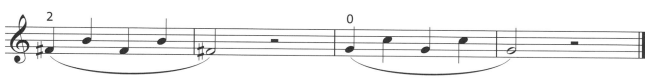

Push the note up by blowing *too – hee* as you compress your lips slightly.

Exercise 3:

Lip flexibilities

Practice lip flexibilities going up and down all seven combinations.

Practice these exercises using all seven valve positions:

These are called **lip flexibilities**.

Pieces for Lesson 15

Skating

Think *too – hee* at the beginning of this one to push up the lip slur.

Home On The Range

The First Noël

Notice the dynamic markings in this next piece. Try to grade the dynamics so that the piece becomes progressively louder, saving some strength for the final 4 bars.

test: *for* Lessons 11 to 15

1. Key signatures

On the staff below, draw the correct key signatures for:

G major   F major   A minor   A major   C major

(4)

2. Dots

Simplify the music on the left using dots to get rid of the ties:

(4)

3. Notes

Write out the following notes with the correct fingering above each note:

G♯, B♭, F♯, D, C♯, A

(6)

4. Terms

What do the following terms mean:

Fermata _____   *Diminuendo* _____

Legato _____   *Mezzo forte* _____

Piano _____   *Staccato* _____

(6)

5. Scale

Write out and play the A melodic minor scale on the staff below:

(5)

Total (25)

warm up:

Hopefully by now you will be in the habit of warming up before each practice session.

Warming up each day will make your practice sessions more productive, help you develop some fundamental techniques for good brass playing, develop strength and stamina which will help you to play longer, louder and higher, and encourage a faster rate of progress.

It is a good idea to stick to one warm-up for a period of time to allow these exercises to develop your muscles in a certain way.

It is also a good idea to change your warm-up from time to time to encourage the development of new techniques to add interest.

Here are a few more exercises to add to your warm-up routine:

1. Lip flexibilities

Repeat these many times using different valve combinations.

Lip slurs develop flexibility and strengthen the muscles around your embouchure.

Remember to make use of vowel sounds.

2. Tongue and valve coordination

Practice this exercise progressively quicker to develop a good rapport between the valves and fingers.

Practice this exercise both tongued and slurred.

3. Speed tonguing

Practice this type of pattern tonguing as quickly as you can—try to play a little quicker each day.

You will soon develop a super-fast tongue!

Practice this pattern on any note you like.

goals:

1. **Intervals and vowel sounds**
2. **Arpeggios**

You have seen how helpful vowel sounds can be to make lip flexibilities easier.

The same technique can be applied to playing all kinds of intervals, big and small.

Exercise 1:

Play the upper note *louder* and *crescendo* through the lower note to generate some extra power for the upper note.

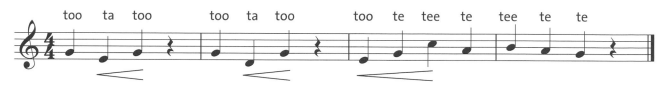

Exercise 2:

Experiment with the "vowel sounds" to find which ones help you leap from note to note.

Blow through the crescendo.

Arpeggios

An *arpeggio* is a short "fanfare" based on the notes that form the chord of a particular key.

Exercise 3: the C major arpeggio

Practice using your vowel sound technique to help leap up and down the arpeggios.

Exercise 4:

C major

B♭ major

D major

A minor

Pieces for Lesson 16

Hop, Skip & Jump

Jumping Beans

Swing Low, Sweet Chariot

Spiritual

71–72

mf

Fine

f

D.C. al Fine

goals:

1. **Articulation**
2. **Note shape**

Refresh your memory and learn some new ways to articulate notes on the trumpet.

Articulation

Articulation describes the way a note is played.

For example, a note can be short or long, and can be played with a hard or soft *attack* .

Exercise 1: *Staccato*

The dot means that each note should be played short. This is called *staccato,* which literally means "detached."
Simply blow a short, sharp burst of air as you say *too.*

Exercise 2: *Accent*

The *accent* indicates that each note should be given a harder attack.
It helps to push a little extra air into each note as well as sharpening your *too.*

Exercise 3: *Soft tonguing*

To articulate softly try using *doo* rather than *too.* Feel how your tongue is slightly further back in the mouth?
To help make an even softer tonguing, imagine that the air starts the note with *hoo* then add a
soft *doo* on top.

Exercise 4: *Tenuto* and *detached* notes

The line indicates that the notes should be played to their full length.
This is called *tenuto,* literally meaning "held." Play these notes with a continuous airstream, blowing from one
note into the next.

Where a line and a dot are used together, the note should be played detached, but not as short as *staccato,*
and should be given emphasis. Think of them as notes that *bounce.* Again, a little push of air helps each one.
Put *too* and *hoo* together.

Note shape

The shape of the start of each note is also very important to good trumpet playing.

Try to avoid the "wa – wa" effect:

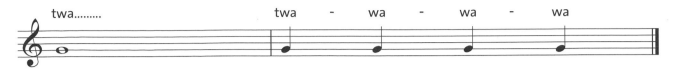

Exercise 5:

Practice starting notes positively like this:

Practice this exercise softly and loudly.

Pieces for Lesson 17

Mango Walk

Can Can

goals:

1. The notes E and E♭
2. E♭ major
3. Lip flexibilities up to E

The note E

E above middle C is part of the open harmonic range, so this note is played on open valves.

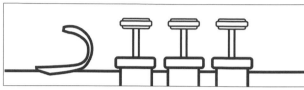

The note E♭

This E♭ is played using the 2nd valve.

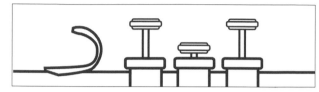

The scale and arpeggio of E♭ major

Notice that the key of E♭ major has 3 flats – B♭, E♭ and A♭.

This means that every B, E and A will be flat throughout the piece.

Here are some more lip flexibilities.

Hopefully by now you are playing lip slurs up to middle C in your warm-up. Take these a step further now by using the next harmonic up. Begin with G on 1 & 3 and work up from there.

Exercise 1:

Practice these slowly at first using the vowel sounds *te* and *eee* and a little push of air with *hee* to help you blow these notes up and down.

Remember where *hoo* comes from in your stomach—give that same push with *hee*.

Compress your lips slightly on the way up and relax again on the way down.

Continue up the valve sequence to C on open valves.

Exercise 2:

Blow through the lip slur. Give a little push from your belly on the way up.

Think *too – eh – oo – o – oo* then *teh – ee – eh – oo – eh* as you go higher.

Use vowel sounds to help push the lip slurs up and down.

Pieces for Lesson 18

When The Saints Go Marching In (E♭)

Home Sweet Home

75

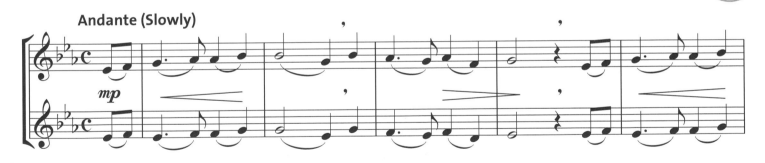

goals:

1. **The note upper F**
2. **Range building**

The note upper F

The note F is played using the same fingering in both octaves: 1st valve.

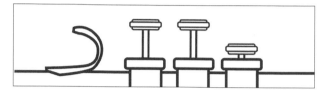

Range building

Trumpet melodies often contain high notes, and this requires strength and stamina.

This exercise develops control of the airstream: experiment with the vowel sounds studied so far to see what works best, and crescendo through each phrase.

Exercise 1:

Blow through the slur.

Practice this exercise often and add another note on top as it becomes easier.

Pieces for Lesson 19

Blue Skies

Reflective

Winding Up

goals:

1. **Musical expression**
2. **D minor scales and arpeggio**
3. **Extreme dynamics**

Musical expression

The trumpet can be a very expressive instrument and there are many ways to give meaning to the music.

To play in a lyrical style we can use a sensitive mixture of all the musical expressions we have learned so far. Use more varied combinations of dynamics, slurs, tempos and articulation to express your musical ideas.

Pieces for Lesson 20

Try to give these two contrasting pieces their own individual character.

Sostenuto means sustained—try to play nice long phrases and gently *crescendo* and *diminuendo* where marked. Give the Rondo some gusto!

From *The Unfinished Symphony*
Schubert

Rondo from Horn Concerto No.4
Mozart

Let's hear the hunting horns calling!

D minor scales and arpeggio

F major and D minor are *relatives* since they share the same key signature.

Exercise 1:

D melodic minor

Exercise 2:

D harmonic minor

Exercise 3:

D minor arpeggio

Extreme Dynamics

Practice these simple exercises to develop strength and control for louder and softer dynamics. *ff* means *double forte* – even louder than forte, and *pp* means *double piano*—even softer than piano.
We need to control the dynamics at both extremes.

Don't blow so loud that it distorts the sound and not so soft that the sound disappears completely.

Exercise 4:

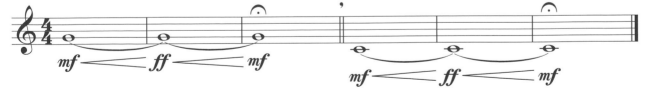

Practice these exercises using different notes to help you develop good dynamic control over your full register.

Exercise 5:

Lesson 20

Pieces for Lesson 20

Greensleeves

79 *Got The Blues*

1. Articulations

Play the following well-known piece, taking care to make all the articulations.

Try to distinguish between each different articulation in your performance.

(6)

2. New keys

Return to page 19 and, using your knowledge of scales and key signatures,

play *When The Saints Go Marching In* in two other major keys of your choice.

(6)

3. Breath control

Play this note with a steady tone, controlling your breath at all times.

You will score one point (up to a maximum of five) for every three seconds held.

(5)

4. Dynamics

Put these dynamic marks in the correct order from softest to loudest:

mf   *p*   *ff*   *mp*   *pp*   *f*

(3)

5. Arpeggios

Play the arpeggios of the following keys:

B♭ major   D major   F major   A minor   E♭ major

(5)

Total (25)

CD backing tracks

1	Tuning note A
2	Virtuoso Performance
3	Buzzing (C) *demonstration*
4	Buzzing (G) *demonstration*
5	Little C & D March *demonstration*
6	Little C & D March *backing only*
7	Little F & G March *demonstration*
8	Little F & G March *backing only*
9	C *duet*
10	G *duet*
11	Lightly Row *demonstration*
12	Lightly Row *backing only*
13	Medieval Dance *duet*
14	Au Clair de la Lune *demonstration*
15	Au Clair de la Lune *backing only*
16	Upidee *duet*
17	When The Saints Go Marching In *demonstration*
18	When The Saints Go Marching In *backing only*
19	Up The Old Vic *demonstration*
20	Up The Old Vic *backing only*
21	Floating Along *demonstration*
22	Floating Along *backing only*
23	Dance *demonstration*
24	Dance *backing only*
25	Sailing Along *duet*
26	Joshua Fought The Battle Of Jericho *demonstration*
27	Joshua Fought The Battle Of Jericho *backing only*
28	Steal Away *demonstration*
29	Steal Away *backing only*
30	Blue Tuesday *duet*
31	Skye Boat Song *demonstration*
32	Skye Boat Song *backing only*
33	Scarborough Fair *duet*

34	When The Saints Go Marching In *demonstration*
35	When The Saints Go Marching In *backing only*
36	Medieval Dance *duet backing only*
37	Au Clair de la Lune *duet*
38	Long Long Ago *demonstration*
39	Long Long Ago *backing only*
40	O Come All Ye Faithful *demonstration*
41	O Come All Ye Faithful *backing only*
42	Yankee Doodle *demonstration*
43	Yankee Doodle *backing only*
44	Hark! The Herald Angels Sing *demonstration*
45	Hark! The Herald Angels Sing *backing only*
46	Auld Lang Syne *demonstration*
47	Auld Lang Syne *backing only*
48	In Dulci Jubilo *demonstration*
49	In Dulci Jubilo *backing only*
50	Oh! Susannah *demonstration*
51	Oh! Susannah *backing only*
52	Deck The Halls *demonstration*
53	Deck The Halls *backing only*
54	Lullaby *duet*
55	Joy To The World *demonstration*
56	Joy To The World *backing only*
57	Mulberry Bush *demonstration*
58	Mulberry Bush *backing only*
59	Spanish Dance *demonstration*
60	Spanish Dance *backing only*
61	Jingle Bells – Jazz Style *demonstration*
62	Jingle Bells – Jazz Style *backing only*

63	Blow The Boogie Woogie *demonstration*
64	Blow The Boogie Woogie *backing only*
65	Believe Me If *demonstration*
66	Believe Me If *backing only*
67	Home On The Range *demonstration*
68	Home On The Range *backing only*
69	The First Noel *demonstration*
70	The First Noel *backing only*
71	Swing Low, Sweet Chariot *demonstration*
72	Swing Low, Sweet Chariot *backing only*
73	Mango Walk *demonstration*
74	Mango Walk *backing only*
75	Home Sweet Home *duet*
76	Blue Skies *demonstration*
77	Blue Skies *backing only*
78	Winding Up *trio*
79	Got The Blues *trio*

How to use the CD

The tuning note on track 1 is a concert A, which sounds B on the trumpet.

After track 2, which gives an idea of how the trumpet can sound, the backing tracks are listed in the order in which they appear in the book. Look for the symbol in the book for the relevant backing track.

Where both parts of a duet are included on the CD, the top part is in one channel, and the bottom part is in the other channel.